太極拳
經論要訣

THE ESSENCE OF T'AI CHI CH'UAN

The Literary Tradition

Translated and Edited
by

Benjamin Pang Jeng Lo

Martin Inn

Robert Amacker

Susan Foe

North Atlantic Books
Berkeley, California

THE ESSENCE OF T'AI CHI CH'UAN: The Literary Tradition

ISBN 0–913028–63–0

Published by
North Atlantic Books
P.O. Box 12327
Berkeley, California 94712

Cover: Legendary founder of T'ai Chi Ch'uan, Chang San-feng
Calligraphy by Benjamin Pang Jeng Lo
Graphic production by Andrew Main
Typeset in Patina by the Open Studio Print Shop, Rhinebeck, N.Y.

Printed in the United States of America

Publication partially supported by the New York State Council on the Arts and the National Endowment for the Arts.

THE ESSENCE OF T'AI CHI CH'UAN: The Literary Tradition is sponsored by the Society for the Study of Native Arts and Sciences, a nonprofit educational corporation whose goals are to develop an educational and crosscultural perspective linking various scientific, social, and artistic fields; to nurture a holistic view of arts, sciences, humanities, and healing; and to publish and distribute literature on the relationship of mind, body, and nature.

12   13   14   15   16   17   18   19 / 99   98   97   96

CONTENTS

PREFACE

Translations should be both poetic and literal, yet frequently one ideal must be sacrificed to the other. In translating literature like the T'ai Chi Ch'uan *Classics*, which is a collection of writings spanning almost one thousand years, there are many problems. For one thing, classical Chinese is terse, even telegraphic. Many characters have both concrete and abstract meanings so even simple sentences resound with allusions and imagery. Each aphorism echoes in the reader's mind, creating overtones which stimulate new ideas and amplify old ones.

For example, in the "T'ai Chi Ch'uan Ching," which is one of the oldest writings, appears the sentence, "the *ch'i* (breath) should be excited, the spirit should be internally gathered." In this context the word which we translate as "excited" has this connotation: if all the oceans in the world were gathered into a box and the box was jiggled, the water would slosh back and forth. This is how the *ch'i* circulates in the body. Yet translating this as "the breath should slosh" is misleading and awkward.

This problem of translating and interpreting the *Classics* has existed all along, for even one thousand years ago, classical Chinese bore little relation to ordinary speech. After the *Four Books* became entrenched as literary models, most writing emulated the style of 400 B.C. The real model of the "T'ai Chi Ch'uan Ching," however, is Sun Tze's *Art of War*. This was also written about 400 B.C., and remains the most concise and illuminating book of military strategy ever written. What Sun Tze's treatise (and its commentaries) did for military battles, the T'ai Chi Ch'uan *Classics* do for individual combat— to authoritatively define and analyze the factors that bring success. In addition, the *Classics* expound a path of development for the body, mind, and spirit.

Because of its lofty goals and profound insights the T'ai Chi Ch'uan *Classics* is considered a book of wisdom. In the Orient if a book which addresses itself to philosophical questions has merit, later scholars add their own commentaries. Over the centuries, as commentary is added to commentary, they come to be accepted as part of the work itself. New ideas are added and old ones are dropped as the text comes under the scrutiny of each succeeding generation. This organic process of addition and deletion tends to glean out the ideas found to be the wisest and most useful so that each proverb is like a telegram from past T'ai Chi Ch'uan practitioners. The present generation must bring to the work the same searching appraisal and creativity.

That we have the *Classics* at all is an historical accident. In the mid-19th Century an old manuscript was found in a salt shop by a scholar who took it to his brother, Wu

Yu-hsiang. Wu (1812-1880) was a student of the famous T'ai Chi family, the Chen clan of northern China. Wu showed the manuscript to his friend and teacher Yang Lu-shan (1800-1873). Yang confirmed the wisdom of the epigrams and interpreted them to Wu, who later wrote the "Expositions and Insights." Both made the *Classics* the literary foundation of their teachings and founded schools which survive to the present day.

Although the actual authorship of the "Ching" is impossible to determine, the epigrams are attributed to Chang San-feng, the legendary founder of T'ai Chi Ch'uan. He is believed to have been a Taoist monk who lived from 1279-1368 A.D., although some believe he lived for more than 250 years. He studied boxing at the Shaolin Temple and then reformed their movements to conform with the Taoist ideas of softness and yielding-ness. The original note on the manuscript said: "This classic was left by the patriarch Chang San-feng of Wu Tang Mountain. He desired the whole world to attain longevity, and not only martial techniques."

One of the major goals of Taoism is health and longevity: "To live forever and be forever young." To achieve this, one must follow the Tao (Way or Path), which means harmonizing with nature and the universe. This harmonization must be both external and internal. T'ai Chi Ch'uan is a method by which external affairs are regulated (self-defense) while the *ch'i* (breath) is cultivated (yoga). The *Classics* refer to both of these ideas. Yet since the framework of T'ai Chi Ch'uan is that of the martial arts, everything in T'ai Chi must stand up to the most rigorous martial analysis. The T'ai Chi

Ch'uan *Classics* is an attempt to state (selectively, even arbitrarily, and by no means exhaustively) the irrevocable principles of Taoism in terms of martial arts. No one can truly say they understand the *Classics* until they can not only offer some interpretation of the statements, but can defend their significance in the specifics of *ch'uan* or boxing. As the understanding of T'ai Chi Ch'uan has changed over the centuries, each practitioner has added his own skill and wisdom.

Since there is no way of determining how much alteration occurred during generations of the T'ai Chi lineage, a few of the epigrams may be innaccurate. For example, in Wu's "Expositions of Insights" appears the statement: "The *li* is released through the back, and the steps follow the bodily changes." *Li* or external strength (see Glossary) is considered undesirable by T'ai Chi boxers. In this context it is almost nonsensical and highly suspect. There is considerable scholarly opinion that this character was originally *chin* (internal force), which is the strength of the sinews, tendons, and muscles. *Chin* is a complex character. Its radical, an identifying component, is the character *li* when it stands alone. Since in addition, the distinction between *li* and *chin* is one which many students find difficulty in making in terms of actual practice, they may have been too timid or confused to question it. Yet to refuse to do so is to lose the value of the *Classics* as a living work.

The chapters in this book are arranged in chronological order. The aphorisms in the "T'ai Chi Ch'uan Ching" are traditionally assigned to Chang San-feng (1279-1386 A.D.). The "T'ai Chi Ch'uan Lun" are thought to have been written by Wang Tsung-yueh, who was the first known successor to Chang San-feng. He introduced T'ai Chi Ch'uan in Honan Province between 1736-1795. The "Expositions and Insights" were written by Wu Yu-hsiang (1812-1880). Li I-yu, who lived in the mid-19th Century, wrote the "Essentials of Form and Push-Hands" and the "Five Character Secret." These are designed to be a practical guide to actual realization of the more philosophical texts, but in fact only yield their secrets to advanced practitioners.

The names and dates of the authors of "Song of the Thirteen Postures" and the "Song of Hand-Pushing" are lost. Incidentally, these are poems and not meant to be sung. Yang Cheng-fu, the author of "Yang's Ten Important Points," was a grandson of Yang Lu-shan. He lived from 1883 to 1936 and was the foremost T'ai Chi boxer of his day, famed throughout China for his softness and martial prowess. His student, Cheng Man-ch'ing (1900-1975) was a Master of the Five Excellences: poetry, painting, calligraphy, medicine, and T'ai Chi Ch'uan. His poem "Song of Form and Function" is translated from his *Thirteen Chapters*. This is the first time it has been published in English.

Because of the seemingly random arrangement of the "Lun," we have somewhat altered the order to facilitate understanding of these frequently cryptic aphorisms. The reader must be careful to note, however, that this order is neither historical nor necessary so he must avoid drawing conclusions based on the progressions of ideas alone. In terms of the individual statements, no license was taken of any kind, the English being the best choice

11

of words which still falls within the literal meaning of the characters.

It is the hope of the authors that readers will not only appreciate the *Classics* for their beauty and wisdom, but will also be stimulated to continue the tradition of adding their own insights and commentaries.

Susan Foe

INTRODUCTION

T'ai Chi Ch'uan began in China several hundred years ago, but the exact date is uncertain. In ancient times teachers taught students privately and the teaching was kept secret. But over the years the historical accuracy of the teaching became impaired as people forgot some things and added others. The exact origin of T'ai Chi Ch'uan was lost. Although people have studied and researched the origin of T'ai Chi, not everyone agrees.

At present there are two main theories concerning the origin of T'ai Chi Ch'uan. One legend is that the hermit Chang San-feng of Wu-tang Mountain invented T'ai Chi at the end of the Yuan and the beginning of the Ming dynasties (1367-1403 A.D.). Some, however, doubt the existence of Chang San-feng. Another theory states that T'ai Chi was first created by Ch'en Wang-t'ing at the end of the Ming and the beginning of the Ch'ing dynasties (1628-1736 A.D.). He founded the Ch'en family T'ai Chi dynasty. In addition to these two popular theories, another idea is that T'ai Chi comes from the end of the Liang and the beginning of the Chen dynasties (550-560 A.D.). Another theory is that it dates from the T'ang dynasty

(705-762 A.D.). These theories are of lesser significance.

In China martial arts are shrouded with a misty curtain. T'ai Chi too, used the "closed door" teaching method, i.e., total secrecy; or the "half-closed door," in other words, people knew what T'ai Chi was, but they didn't know the method. In either case, the transmission was directly from grand-teacher to teacher, teacher to students. But for those standing outside the door, the content was mysterious. So until we discover new evidence concerning the origin of T'ai Chi Ch'uan, we cannot really know.

The most reliable record begins with Ch'en Ch'ang-hsien (1771-1853 A.D.) of Ch'en Chia K'ou in Wen-hsien (Honan Province) during the Ch'ien-lung reign (1736-1796) of the Ch'ing Dynasty. According to the Ch'en family records, although many generations of the Ch'en family practiced the art, it is Yang Lu-shan (1799-1872), the disciple of Ch'en Ch'ang-hsien and the originator of Yang Style T'ai Chi, who first spread the art throughout China with acclaim. After studying with Ch'en, he went to Peking and engaged in many martial bouts with famous masters, winning the nickname, "Yang of No Equal." Contemporary with Yang Lu-shan was Wu Yu-hsiang (1812-1880), who was a student of Ch'en Ching-ping of the same Ch'en clan. Wu then started the Wu school, and that is why today there are three main schools of T'ai Chi: the Ch'en, Yang, and Wu. All practitioners descend from these lines. The Yang school is the most widespread because Yang Lu-shan reached outside his own clansmen to accept outsiders as students. Yang's sons, Pan-hou (1837-1892) and Chien-hou (1839-1917), were both great masters. Chien-hou's son, Yang Cheng-fu (1883-1936), was a famous teacher who continued to spread T'ai Chi throughout China. After Yang Cheng-fu died, his students followed his desire and continued to disseminate T'ai Chi openly. Their hard work made it known not only in China, but in the whole world.

Although the main transmission was oral, some of the past masters did leave a record of their insights. That record of the theory and principles is the *Classics* of T'ai Chi Ch'uan. All of the students who want to develop their skills must follow these precepts.

One question students often ask is, "How do you know what you are doing is right?" To students, this question is important because no one wants to learn the wrong thing. If you work for many years incorrectly, it is a bitter experience. I remember thirty years ago when I asked my late teacher, Cheng Man-ch'ing, the same question. He said, "When you practice the form, once you move, you should follow the T'ai Chi *Classics*. If the movement follows the *Classics*, it is correct." After many years of practice, I really feel that the former practitioners' experience is a treasure. So when a student asks me this question, I naturally answer as my teacher did.

The next question is, "Where can we read an English translation of the *Classics*?" Until now, this question has been hard to answer. I read some English translations, but the meaning seemed incomplete. My three colleagues agreed to attempt a new translation with me. We started in 1976 to work on the *Classics* one by one. We discussed and debated each word many times. We worked intermittently but steadily for two years, and finished in the beginning of 1978. We feel we have done our best, but the translation was not easy. Translating the *Classics* is different from translating other books because it is written in the classical style, and the translator must have some knowledge of classical Chinese. Also, the translator must be experienced in T'ai Chi Ch'uan. Otherwise, the choice of words won't reflect the actual meaning. Despite our best efforts, some errors may remain. I hope that the readers will help us in correcting for future editions.

Benjamin Pang Jeng Lo

太極拳經 張三丰

T'AI CHI CH'UAN

CHING

by

Chang San-feng

In motion
all parts of the body must be
light
nimble
and strung together.

The *ch'i* (breath) should be excited,
the *shen* (spirit) should be internally gathered.

Let the postures be without
breaks or holes,
hollows or projections,
or discontinuities and continuities of form.

The motion should be rooted in the feet,
released through the legs,
controlled by the waist,
and manifested through the fingers.

The feet, legs and waist
must act together simultaneously,
so that while stepping forward or back
the timing and position are correct.

If the timing and position are not correct,
the body becomes disordered,
and the defect must be sought
in the legs and waist.

Up or down,
front or back,
left or right, are all the same.

These are all *i* (mind) and not external.

If there is up, there is down;
if there is forward, then there is backward;
if there is left, then there is right.

If the *i* wants to move up,
it contains at the same time
the downward idea.

By alternating the force
of pulling and pushing,
the root is severed
and the object is quickly toppled,
without a doubt.

Insubstantial and substantial
should be clearly differentiated.

One place
has insubstantiality and substantiality;
every place
has the same insubstantiality and substantiality.

All parts of the body are strung together
without the slightest break.

Ch'ang Ch'uan (T'ai Chi Ch'uan)
is like a great river
rolling on unceasingly.

P'eng (wardoff), *lu* (rollback),
chi (press), *an* (push),
ts'ai (pull), *lieh* (split),
tsou (elbow), *k'ao* (shoulder),
are the eight trigrams.

Step forward, step back,
look left, look right,
and central equilibrium
are the five elements.

P'eng, lu, chi, an, are *ch'ien, k'un, k'an, li,*
and are the four cardinal directions.
Ts'ai, lieh, tsou, k'ao, are *sun, chen, tui, ken,*
and are the four diagonal directions.

Step forward, step back,
look left, look right,
and central equilibrium
are metal, wood, water, fire and earth.

Together
these comprise the thirteen postures.

(Original note states:) This classic was left by the patriarch
Chang San-feng of Wu Tang Mountain. He desired the
whole world to attain longevity, and not only martial
techniques.

太極拳論

王宗岳

T'AI CHI CH'UAN

LUN

by

Wang Tsung-yueh

T'ai Chi
comes from
Wu Chi
and is the mother of *Yin* and *Yang*.

In motion it separates;
in stillness they fuse.

It is not excessive or deficient;
accordingly when it bends,
it then straightens.

When the opponent is hard
and I am soft,
it is called *tsou* (yielding).

When I follow the opponent
and he becomes backed up,
it is called *nien* (adherence).

If the opponent's movement is quick,
then quickly respond;
if his movement is slow,
then follow slowly.

Although the changes are numerous,
the principle
that pervades them
is only
one.

From familiarity with the correct touch,
one gradually comprehends *chin* (internal force);
from the comprehension of *chin*
one can reach wisdom.

Without long practice
one cannot suddenly understand it.

Effortlessly the *chin* reaches the headtop.

Let the *ch'i* (breath) sink to the *tan t'ien*.

Don't lean in any direction;
suddenly appear,
suddenly disappear.

Empty the left wherever a pressure appears,
and similarly the right.

If the opponent raises up I seem taller;
if he sinks down, then I seem lower;
advancing, the distance seems
incredibly longer;
retreating, the distance seems
exasperatingly short.

(So light an object as) a feather
cannot be placed, and
(so small an insect as) a fly
cannot alight
on any part of the body.

The opponent doesn't know me;
I alone know him.

To become a peerless boxer results from this.

There are many boxing arts.

Although they use different forms,
for the most part they don't go beyond
the strong oppressing the weak,
and the slow resigning to the swift.

The strong defeating the weak
and the slow hands ceding to swift hands
are all results
of the physical instinctive capacity
and not of well trained techniques.

From the sentence "A force of four ounces
deflects a thousand pounds"
we know that the technique
is not accomplished with strength.

The spectacle of an old person
defeating a group of young people,
how can it be due to swiftness?

Stand like a balance and
rotate actively like a wheel.

Sinking to one side is responsive;
being double-weighted is sluggish (stagnant).

Anyone who has spent years of practice
and still cannot neutralize,
and is always controlled by his opponent,
has not apprehended
the fault of double-weightedness.

To avoid this fault
one must know *yin* and *yang*.

Yin and *yang*
mutually aid and change each other.

Then you can say
you understand *chin* (internal strength).
After you understand *chin*,
the more practice, the more skill.

Silently treasure up knowledge
and turn it over in the mind.
Gradually you can do as you like.

Originally it is giving up yourself
to follow others.
Most people mistakenly give up the near
to seek the far.
It is said, "Missing it by a little
will lead many miles astray."

The practitioner must carefully study.

This is the *Lun*.

EXPOSITIONS OF INSIGHTS

INTO THE PRACTICE

OF THE

THIRTEEN POSTURES

by

Wu Yu-hsiang

The *hsin* (mind)
mobilizes the *ch'i* (breath).

Make the *ch'i* sink calmly;
then it gathers
and permeates the bones.

The *ch'i* mobilizes the body.

Make it move smoothly,
then it easily follows
(the direction of) the *hsin*.

The *i* (mind) and *ch'i* (breath)
must change agilely,
then there is an excellence of
roundness and smoothness.

This is called
"the change of insubstantial and substantial."

The *hsin* (mind) is the commander,
the *ch'i* (breath) the flag,
and the waist the banner.

The waist is like the axle
and the *ch'i* is like the wheel.

The *ch'i* (breath) is always nurtured
without harm.

Let the *ch'i* move
as in a pearl with nine passages *(chiu ch'u chu)*
without breaks
so that there is no part (of the body)
it cannot reach.

In moving
the *ch'i* sticks to the back
and permeates the spine.

It is said "First in the *hsin* (mind),
then in the body."

The abdomen relaxes,
then the *ch'i* (breath) sinks into the bones.

The *shen* (spirit) is relaxed
and the body calm.

It is always in the *hsin*.

Being able to breathe (properly)
leads to agility.

The softest
will then become
the strongest.

When the *ching shen* (spirit) is raised,
there is no fault
of stagnancy and heaviness.

This is called suspended headtop.

Inwardly
make the *ching shen* firm,
and outwardly
exhibit calmness and peace.

Throughout the body,
the *i* (mind) relies on the *ching shen* (spirit),
not on the *ch'i* (breath).

If it relied on the *ch'i*,
it would become stagnant.

If there is *ch'i*,
there is no *li* (external strength).

If there is no *ch'i*,
there is pure steel.

The *chin* (internal strength) is *sung* (relaxed),
but not *sung;*
it will extend,
but is not extended.

The *chin* is broken,
but the *i* (mind) is not.

The *chin* is stored (having a surplus)
by means of the curved.

The *li* (force) is released by the back,
and the steps follow the changes of the body.

The mobilization of the *chin* (internal strength)
is like refining steel a hundred times over.

There is nothing hard
it cannot destroy.

Store up the *chin* (internal strength)
like drawing a bow.

Mobilize the *chin*
like pulling silk from a cocoon.

Release the *chin*
like releasing the arrow.

To *fa chin* (release energy),
sink,
relax completely,
and aim in one direction!

In the curve seek the straight,
store,
then release.

Be as still as a mountain,
move like a great river.

The upright body
must be stable and comfortable
to be able to support (force from)
the eight directions.

Walk like a cat.

Remember, when moving,
there is no place that doesn't move.

When still,
there is no place that isn't still.

First seek extension,
then contraction;
then it can be fine and subtle.

It is said "if others don't move,
I don't move.

If others move slightly,
I move first."

To withdraw is then to release,
to release is to withdraw.

In discontinuity
there is still continuity.

In advancing and returning
there must be folding.

Going forward and back
there must be changes.

The form is like that
of a falcon about to seize a rabbit,
and the *shen* (spirit) is like that
of a cat about to catch a rat.

SONG OF THE

THIRTEEN POSTURES

by

Unknown Author

The thirteen postures
   should not be taken lightly;
The source of the postures lies in the waist.

Be mindful of the insubstantial
   and substantial changes;
The *ch'i* (breath) spreads throughout
   without hindrance.

Being still, when attacked by the opponent,
   be tranquil and move in stillness;
(My) changes caused by the opponent
   fill him with wonder.

Study the function of each posture
    carefully and with deliberation;
To achieve the goal is very easy.

Pay attention to the waist at all times;
Completely relax the abdomen
    and the *ch'i* (breath) rises up.

When the coccyx is straight,
    the *shen* (spirit) goes through to the headtop.

To make the whole body light and agile
    suspend the headtop.

Carefully study.

Extension and contraction, opening and closing,
   should be natural.

To enter the door and be shown the way,
   you must be orally taught.
The practice is uninterrupted,
   and the technique (achieved) by self study.

Speaking of the body and its function,
   what is the standard?

The *i* (mind) and *ch'i* (breath) are king,
   and the bones and muscles are the court.

Think over carefully what the final purpose is:
to lengthen life and maintain youth.

The Song consists of 140 characters;
Each character is true
and the meaning is complete.

If you do not study in this manner,
then you'll waste your time and sigh.

打手歌

SONG OF

HAND-PUSHING

by

Unknown Author

Be conscientious in *p'eng* (wardoff),
  lu (rollback), *chi* (press) and *an* (push).

Upper and lower coordinate,
  and others find it difficult to penetrate.

Let others attack with great force;
Use four ounces
  to deflect a thousand pounds.

Attract to emptiness and discharge;
Attach *(chan, lien, t'ieh, sui)*
  without losing the attachment.

五字訣

李亦畬

FIVE CHARACTER

SECRET

by

Li I-yu

CALM

The mind should be calm. If it is not, one cannot concentrate, and when the arm is raised, (whether) forward or back, left or right, it is completely without certain direction. Therefore it is necessary to maintain a calm mind. In beginning to move, you cannot control (it) by yourself. The entire mind must (also) experience and comprehend the movements of the opponent. Accordingly, when (the movement) bends, it then straightens, without disconnecting or resisting. Do not extend or retreat by yourself. If my opponent has *li* (strength), I also have *li*, but my *li* is previous (in exact anticipation of his). If the opponent does not have *li*, I am also without it *(li)*, but my mind is still previous. It is necessary to be continually mindful; to whatever part (of the body) is touched the mind should go. You must discover the information by non-discrimination and non-resistance. Follow this method, and in one year, or a half-year, you will instinctively find it in your body. All of this means use *i* (mind), not *chin* (internal force). After a long time the opponent will be controlled by me and I will not be controlled by him.

If the body is clumsy, then in advancing or retreating it cannot be free; therefore it must be agile. Once you raise your arm, you cannot appear clumsy. The moment the force of the opponent touches my skin and hair, my mind is already penetrating his bones. When holding up the arms, the ch'i (breath) is threaded together continuously. When the left side is heavy, it then empties, and the right side is already countering. When the right is heavy, it empties, and the left is already countering. The ch'i is like a wheel, and the whole body must mutually coordinate. If there is any uncoordinated place, the body becomes disordered and weak. The defect is to be found in the waist and legs. First the mind is used to order the body. Follow the opponent and not yourself (your own inclination). Later your body can follow your mind, and you can control yourself and still follow the opponent. When you only follow yourself, you are clumsy, but when you follow (coordinate with) the opponent, you are lively. When you can follow your opponent, then your hands can distinguish and weigh accurately the amount of his force, and measure the distance of his approach with no mistake. Advancing and retreating, everywhere (the coordination) is perfect. After studying for a long time, your technique will become skillful.

BREATH
To Gather the Ch'i

If the ch'i is dispersed, then it is not stored (accumulated) and is easy to scatter. Let the ch'i penetrate the spine and the inhalation and exhalation be smooth and unimpeded throughout the entire body. The inhalation closes and gathers, the exhalation opens and discharges. Because the inhalation can naturally raise and also uproot the opponent, the exhalation can naturally sink down and also discharge *(fa fang)* him. This is by means of the *i* (mind), not the *li* (strength) mobilizing the *ch'i* (breath).

INTERNAL FORCE
The Complete *Chin*

The *chin* of the (whole) body, through practice becomes one unit. Distinguish clearly between substantial and insubstantial. To *fa chin* (discharge) it is necessary to have root. The *chin* starts from the foot, is commanded by the waist, and manifested in the fingers, and discharged through the spine and back. One must completely raise the spirit (pay attention) at the moment when the opponent's *chin* is just about to manifest, but has not yet been released. My *chin* has then already met his *(chin)*, not late, not early. It is like using a leather (tinder) to start a fire, or like a fountain gushing forth. (In) going forward or stepping back, there is not even the slightest disorder. In the curve seek the straight, store, then discharge; then you are able to follow your hands and achieve a beneficial result. This is called borrowing force to strike the opponent or using four ounces to deflect a thousand pounds.

SPIRIT
Shen Concentrated

Having the above four, then you can return to concentrated spirit: if the spirit is concentrated, then it is (continuous and) uninterrupted, and the practice of *ch'i* (breath) returns to the *shen* (spirit). The manifestation of *ch'i* moves with agility. (When) the spirit is concentrated, opening and closing occur appropriately, and the differentiation of substantial and insubstantial is clear. If the left is insubstantial, the right is substantial, and vice-versa. Insubstantial does not mean completely without strength. The manifestation of the *ch'i* must be agile. Substantial does not mean completely limited. The spirit must be completely concentrated. It is important to be completely in the mind (heart) and waist, and not outside.

Not being outside or separated, force is borrowed from the opponent, and the *ch'i* is released from the spine. How can the *ch'i* discharge from the spine? It sinks downward from the two shoulders, gathers to the spine, and pours to the waist. This is *ch'i* from up to down and is called "closed". From the waist the *ch'i* mobilizes to the spine, spreads to the two arms and flows to the fingers. This is *ch'i* from down to up and is called "opened". Closed is gathering, and opened is discharging. When you know opening and closing, then you know *yin* and *yang*. Reaching this level your skill will progress with the days and you can do as you wish.

ESSENTIALS

OF THE PRACTICE

OF FORM

AND PUSH-HANDS

by

Li I-yu

Formerly people said: being able to attract to emptiness, you can use four ounces to deflect a thousand pounds. Not being able to attract to emptiness, you cannot deflect a thousand pounds. The words are simple, but the meaning is complete. The beginner cannot understand it. Here I add some words to explain it. If someone is ambitious to learn this art, he can find some way to enter it and every day he will have improvement.

Desiring to attract to emptiness and use four ounces to deflect a thousand pounds, first you must know yourself and others. If you want to know yourself and others, you must give up yourself and follow others. If you give up yourself and follow others, first you must have the correct timing and position. To obtain the correct timing and position, you must first make your body one unit. Desiring to make the body one unit, you must first eliminate hollows and protuberances. To make the whole body without breaks or holes, you must first have the *shen* (spirit) and *ch'i* (breath) excited and expanded. If you want the *shen* and *ch'i* activated and expanded, you must first raise the spirit (pay attention) and the *shen* should not be unfocussed. To have your *shen* not unfocussed, you must first have the *shen* and *ch'i* gather and penetrate the bones. Desiring the *shen* and *ch'i* to penetrate the bones, first you must strengthen the two thighs and loosen the two shoulders and let the *ch'i* sink down.

The *chin* (internal force) raises from the feet, changes in the legs, is stored in the chest, moved in the shoulders and commanded in the waist. The upper part connects to the two arms and the lower part follows the legs. It changes inside. To gather is to close and to release is to open. If it is quiet, it is completely still. Still means to close. In closing there is opening. If it is moving, everything moves. Moving is open. In opening there is closing. When the body is touched it revolves freely. There is nowhere that does not obtain power. Then you can attract to emptiness and use four ounces to deflect a thousand pounds.

Practicing the form every day is the *kung fu* (way of practicing) of knowing yourself. When you start to practice, first ask yourself, "Did my whole body follow the previous principles or not?" If one little place didn't follow (them), then correct it immediately. Therefore, in practicing the form we want slowness not speed.

Push hands is the *kung fu* of knowing others. As for movement and stillness, although it is to know others, you must still ask yourself. If you arrange yourself well, when others touch you, you don't move a hair. Follow the opportunity and meet his *chin* (internal force) and let him naturally fall outward. If you feel someplace (in your body) is powerless, it is double-weighted and unchanging. You must seek (the defect) in *yin* and *yang*, opening and closing. Know yourself and know others: in one hundred battles you will win one hundred times.

YANG'S TEN

IMPORTANT POINTS

by

Yang Cheng-fu

Commentary by

Chen Wei-ming

1. **The head should be upright so the** *shen* **(spirit) can reach the headtop.** Don't use *li* (strength), or the neck will be stiff and the *ch'i* (breath) and blood cannot flow through. It is necessary to have a natural and lively feeling. If the spirit cannot reach the headtop, it cannot raise.

2. **Sink the chest and pluck up the back.** The chest is depressed naturally inward so that the *ch'i* (breath) can sink to the *tan t'ien*. Don't project the chest: the *ch'i* gets stuck there and the body becomes top-heavy. The heel will be too light and can be uprooted. Pluck up the back and the *ch'i* sticks to the back; depress the chest and you can pluck up the back. Then you can discharge force through the spine. You will be a peerless boxer.

3. *Sung* **(relax) the waist.** The waist is the commander of the whole body. If you can *sung* the waist, then the two legs will have power and the lower part will be firm and stable. Substantial and insubstantial change, and this is based on the turning of the waist. It is said "the source of the postures lies in the waist. If you cannot get power, seek the defect in the legs and waist."

4. **Differentiate insubstantial and substantial.** This is the first thing of all in T'ai Chi Ch'uan. If the weight of the whole body is resting on the right leg, then the right leg is substantial and the left leg is insubstantial, and vice versa. When you can separate substantial and insubstantial, you can turn lightly without using strength. If you cannot separate (them), the step is heavy and slow. The stance is not firm and can be easily thrown off balance.

5. **Sink the shoulders and elbows.** The shoulders will be completely relaxed and open. If you cannot relax and sink, the two shoulders will be "uptight." The *ch'i* (breath) will follow them up and the whole body cannot get power. "Sink the elbows" means the elbows go down and relax. If the elbows raise, the shoulders are not able to sink and you cannot discharge people far. The (discharge) is close to the broken force of the external schools.

6. **Use mind and not force.** The T'ai Chi Ch'uan *Classics* say, "all of this means use *i* (mind) and not *li* (force)." In practicing T'ai Chi Ch'uan the whole body relaxes. Don't let one ounce of force remain in the blood vessels, bones, and ligaments to tie yourself up. Then you can be agile and able to change. You will be able to turn freely and easily. Doubting this (not using *li*), how can you increase your power?

The body has meridians like the ground has ditches and trenches. If not obstructed, the water can flow. If the meridian is not closed, the *ch'i* (breath) goes through. If the whole body has hard force and it fills up the meridians, the *ch'i* and blood stop and the turning is not smooth and agile. Just pull one hair and the whole body is off-balance. If you use *i*, not *li*, then the *i* goes to a place (in the body) and the *ch'i* follows it. The *ch'i* and the blood circulate. If you do this every day and never stop, after a long time you will have *nei chin* (real internal force). The T'ai Chi Ch'uan *Classics* say, "when you are extremely soft, then you become extremely hard and strong." Someone who has extremely good T'ai Chi Ch'uan *kung fu* has arms like iron wrapped with cotton and the weight is very heavy. As for those who practice the external schools, when they use *li*, they reveal *li*. When they don't use *li*, they are too light and floating. Their *chin* (internal force) is external and locked together. The *li* of the external schools is easily led and moved, and not to be esteemed.

87

7. **Upper and lower mutually follow.** The T'ai Chi Ch'uan *Classics* say "the motion should be rooted in the feet, released through the legs, controlled by the waist and manifested through the fingers." Everything is the same (acts in one breath). When the hand, waist and foot move together, the eyes follow. If one part doesn't follow, the whole body is disordered.

8. **Inside and outside coordinate.** In the practice of T'ai Chi Ch'uan the main thing is the spirit. Therefore it is said "the spirit is the commander and the body is subordinate." If you can raise the spirit, then the movements will be naturally agile. The postures are not beyond insubstantial and substantial, opening and closing. That which is called open means not only the hands and feet are open, but the mind is also open. That which is called closed means not only the hands and feet are closed, but the mind is also closed. When you can make the inside and outside become one, then it becomes complete.

9. **It is mutually joined and unbroken.** As to the external schools, their *chin* (internal force) is the Latter Heaven brute *chin*. Therefore it is finite. There are connections and breaks. (During the breaks) the old force is exhausted and the new force has not yet been born. At these moments it is very easy for others to take advantage. T'ai Chi Ch'uan uses *i* (mind) and not *li* (force). From beginning to end it is continuous and not broken. It is circular and again resumes. It revolves and has no limits. The original *Classics* say it is "like a great river rolling on unceasingly," and that the circulation of *chin* is "like pulling silk." They all talk about being connected together.

10. **Seek stillness in movement.** The external schools assume jumping about is good and they use all their energy. That is why after practice everyone pants. T'ai Chi Ch'uan uses stillness to control movement. Although one moves, there is also stillness. Therefore in practicing the form, slower is better. If it is slow, the inhalation and exhalation are long and deep and the *ch'i* sinks to *tan t'ien*. Naturally there is no injurious practice such as engorgement of the blood vessels. The learner should be careful to comprehend it. Then you will get the real meaning.

SONG OF FORM

AND FUNCTION

by

Cheng Man-ch'ing

T'ai Chi Ch'uan.

Thirteen postures.

The marvel lies in the two *ch'i* divided into
Yin and *Yang*.

It transforms the myriad and returns to
the One.

Returns to the One.

T'ai Chi Ch'uan.

The *Liang I* (Two Primordial Powers)
and the *Sze Hsiang* (Four Manifestations)
are chaos and boundless.

To ride the winds
how about suspending the headtop?

I have some words to reveal now
to those who can know.

If the *yung ch'uan* (bubbling well) has no root
and the waist has no commander,
studying hard till death will be of no help.

The form and function are mutually connected
and nothing more.

The *hao jan chih ch'i* (Great *Ch'i*)
can be conducted to the hand.

Wardoff, rollback,
press, push,
pull, split,
elbow, shoulder.

Step forward, step back,
look left, look right,
central equilibrium.

Not neutralizing it naturally neutralizes,
not yielding it naturally yields.

(When) the foot wants to advance
first shift backwards.

The body is like a floating cloud.

In push-hands the hands are not needed.

The whole body is a hand
and the hand is not a hand.

But the mind must stay
in the place it should be.

GLOSSARY

Chan, Lien, T'ieh, Sui: These refer to adherence, the "sticking" aspect of T'ai Chi Ch'uan. *Chan* and *lien* are vertical adhering movements, lifting from above and supporting from below, respectively. *T'ieh* is adherence in horizontal motion, and *sui* is adherence from the rear.

Ch'i: Breath or breath energy. In an individual's development, the *ch'i* which one is born with or receives from ones parents is called "former heaven" or pre-natal *ch'i*. After birth one begins to use up this *ch'i*, replacing it (incompletely) with *ch'i* derived from food or air. This is called "latter heaven" or post-natal *ch'i*. Whenever there is a transformation of energy it is possible to characterize it as *ch'i*.

Chin: One of the main objectives of T'ai Chi Ch'uan (and of many martial arts) is the development of *chin*, or internal force. It is contrasted with *li*, which refers to muscular contraction and release. *Chin* is said to develop its power from the muscles and sinews, rather than from binding together and striking with the bones. *Chin* is developed through circular changes, while the flexations of *li* describe straight lines.

Chiu Ch'u Chu: A pearl with nine passages. The number nine is a metaphor for a complex maze of channels through which the *ch'i* must wind to reach every part of the body.

Fa Chin: To release internal force *(chin).*

Fa Fang: To discharge.

Hao Jan Chih Ch'i: Great *Ch'i.* The universal life force inherent in all things. This concept is from the *Book of Mencius.*

Hsin: The essential mind which produces the *i* (idea or will).

I: Mind or idea. *I* and *ch'i* are separate concepts but are almost inseparable in function. One of the objectives of T'ai Chi Ch'uan is to make the *ch'i* or breath energy follow the dictates of the *i,* or mind. In practice the force of will is replaced by the entertaining of an idea, which gradually becomes more and more sensitive to the opponent's changes.

Kung Fu: Achievement of technique or skill.

Li: Using the muscles to bind the bones together into a rigid framework. This habit, and the subsequent use of this rigid framework to strike or push, is antithetical to the techniques of T'ai Chi Ch'uan.

Liang I: Two primordial Powers, i.e., Heaven and Earth, *Yin* and *Yang,* which are the cosmological forces creating all things. The *Liang I* evolved from *T'ai Chi* and is symbolized by a broken and unbroken line. From these the *Sze Hsiang* evolved and then the eight trigrams. (See: *Pa Kua* and *Sze Hsiang.*)

Nien: Adherence or sticking power. When the touch is balanced so that every point of contact with the opponent is equalized, this is called adherence.

Pa Kua: Literally, eight trigrams. The trigrams consist of all the combinations of broken and unbroken lines (binary system) in three positions, as follows:

☰ *Ch'ien*	☷ *K'un*	☵ *K'an*	☲ *Li*
☳ *Chen*	☴ *Sun*	☶ *Ken*	☱ *Tui*

Shen: Spirit; having almost exactly the same connotations as the English term.

Sung: To relax and sink. A distinction should be made between the relaxation of the whole body and a limp or flaccid condition of the body. When the head is picked up, the joints are thrown open and the relaxation of the body is uniform.

Sze Hsiang: Four Manifestations. Four diagrams denoting the evolution of the cosmos from *Yin* and *Yang* to the eight trigrams.

— —		———	
Yin I		*Yang* I	
==	==	==	———
———	———	———	———
T'ai Yin	*Hsiao Yang*	*Hsiao Yin*	*T'ai Yang*

T'ai Chi: The "Supreme Ultimate," a concept in Chinese philosophy denoting the evolution of the cosmos from the primordial state of void *(Wu Chi)* into two antithetical forces, *Yin* and *Yang*. The *T'ai Chi* concept is represented by the familiar *Yin* and *Yang* circle. (See: *Wu Chi.*)

T'ai Chi Ch'uan: Literally, Great Ultimate Boxing. Its principles are based on the *T'ai Chi T'u* or traditional *Yin Yang* circle, hence the name T'ai Chi Ch'uan. *Ch'uan* means fist or boxing and generally refers to all forms of exercise based on the martial arts, e.g., *Shaolin Ch'uan* (boxing of the *Shao-lin* Temple), *Hsing-i Ch'uan*, etc. T'ai Chi Ch'uan was originally known as the "inner school" of boxing or *nei chia*. It was later changed to *T'ai Chi Ch'uan* to distinguish it from other pugilistic descendants of the *nei chia* school. T'ai Chi Ch'uan was also known at one time as *Ch'ang Ch'uan*, or "long boxing."

Tan T'ien: The physical center of the body. It is located approximately two inches below the navel. In T'ai Chi Ch'uan, it is the center for both movement and meditation.

T'i Fang: To uproot and discharge ones opponent. It is the culmination of all the other techniques of push hands. The opponent must be moved without distortion and both of his feet must leave the ground and return together.

Wu Chi: A philosophical concept describing the primordial state of the universe that gives birth to the *T'ai Chi* or *Yin Yang* polarity. This void or nothingness *(Wu Chi)* is represented by the empty circle.

Yin Yang: Originally *Yin* meant the dark shadowed side of a mountain (the northern slope), and *Yang* meant the bright illuminated side (the southern slope). Out of this developed the correspondences of soft and hard, negative and positive, passive and active, female and male. *Yin* and *Yang* are not considered opposing concepts but are really complementary parts of the same whole.

Yung Ch'uan: Bubbling well. The center of the foot where the root lies.